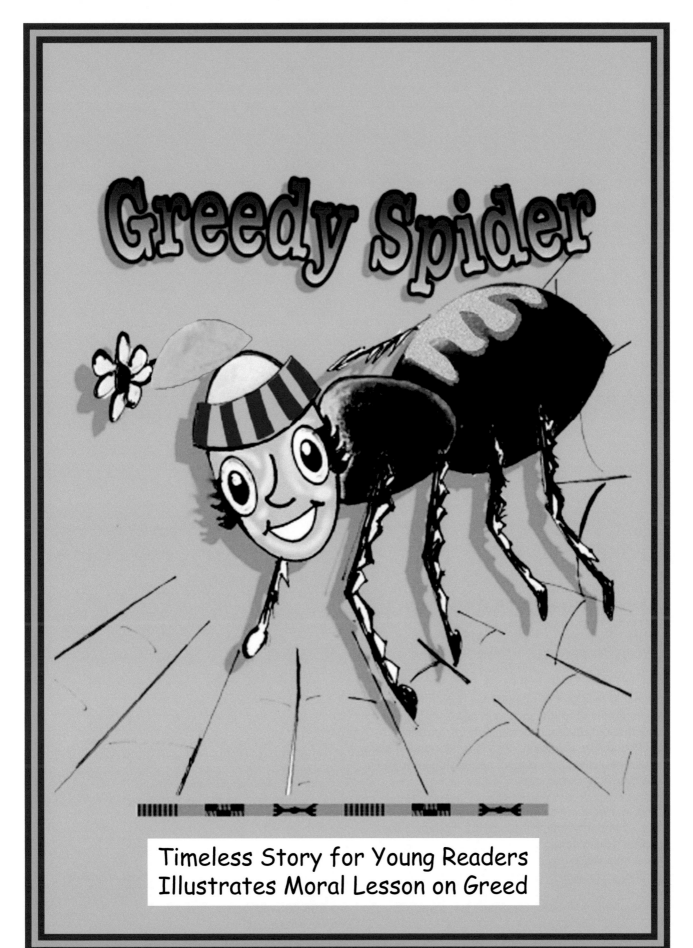

Greedy Spider

Timeless Story for Young Readers
Illustrates Moral Lesson on Greed

To order additional copies of this book, contact:
Xlibris
1-888-795-4274
www.Xlibris.com
Orders@Xlibris.com

Greedy Spider

The story is set in Nyantro, a small village on a rolling hill 55 miles outside Greenville, Sinoe County, Liberia. My grandfather has told and retold this story to me and the children of Nyantro. It was passed on to him after being handed down for more than 700 years.

Bakeh N. Wleh Nagbe, Sr.

Sakontant

Sakontant is the name given to the spider by
the Kru tribe of Liberia.

The Greedy Spider wove day and night. Night and day. She wove beautiful silk threads, which stretched from one bold branch to another.

Her house of silk was a marvel for all in the forest to see as it caught the glistening rays of sunlight and beams of moonlight day after day and night after night.

But, the forest creatures knew that they could only watch from afar, for if they got too close, they could well become breakfast, lunch, dinner or even a snack for Greedy Spider! Her home was also a trap, in which she could ensnare her prey.

Greedy Spider could hang upside down from a thread to catch her prey, and then wind herself back upon the web by the same thread. All of the other creatures envied her and wished for homes as lovely as hers.

One fall day, Greedy Spider was busily spinning her web in the morning sun when Mantis stopped by to say hello on his way to the market.

"Oh, what a beautiful web you weave," he observed. "Yes, it is beautiful," agreed Greedy Spider.

"Will you join me and my family for Thanksgiving dinner?" asked Mantis.

Oh, yes," she hastily answered. "At what time shall I arrive?"

"I'll let you know," Mantis said. He was overjoyed that she had accepted the invitation.

"Tie a rope around my waist and pull it when dinner is ready," Greedy Spider suggested.

Greedy Spider was even happier
than Mantis because she did not have
to prepare the Thanksgiving feast.
She returned to her work of weaving
thinking about the meal that would be
hers on Thanksgiving Day!

It so happened that Greedy Spider was spinning her web in the noonday sun when Hamster stopped to say hello on his way home for lunch.

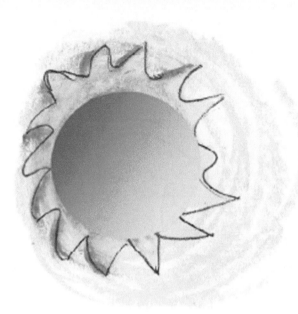

"Oh, what a gorgeous web you weave," he admiringly said. "Yes, it is gorgeous," replied Greedy Spider.

"Will you join me and my family for Thanksgiving dinner?" Hamster asked.

"Oh, yes," she quickly responded. "At what time shall I arrive?"

"I'll let you know," Hamster said. He was delighted that she had accepted his invitation.

"Tie a rope around my waist and pull it when dinner is ready," Greedy Spider suggested.

Now, Greedy Spider was even more excited than Hamster because she had not one, but two invitations for a Thanksgiving feast. And, she was going to eat at both feasts, as a greedy spider might do!

At sunset, Greedy Spider was admiring the good work she had done, when two Snails stopped to say hello on their way home at the end of the day.

"Oh, what a splendid web you weave," the snails proclaimed.

"Yes, it is splendid," replied Greedy Spider.

"Will you join me and my family for Thanksgiving dinner?" asked the two Snails.

"Oh, yes," she eagerly responded. "At what time shall I arrive?"

"We'll let you know," the two Snails said. They were overjoyed she had accepted their invitation.

"Tie a rope around my waist and pull it when dinner is ready," directed Greedy Spider.

Now, Greedy Spider was more thrilled than ever because she had not one, not two, but three invitations for a Thanksgiving feast. And, she was going to eat at all three feasts, as a greedy spider might do!

As the moon in its gentle embrace began to put the forest to sleep, Greedy Spider was preparing for bed when Rabbit stopped to say hello on his evening hop.

"Oh, what a magnificent web you weave," he gleefully exclaimed.

"Yes, it is magnificent," answered Greedy Spider. "Will you join me and my family for Thanksgiving dinner?" asked Rabbit.

"Oh, yes," she responded excitedly. "At what time shall I arrive?" "I'll let you know," Rabbit said. He was so pleased that she had accepted.

"Tie a rope around my waist and pull it when dinner is ready," said Greedy Spider.

Now, Greedy Spider was even more thrilled than Rabbit because she had not one, not two, not three, but four invitations for a Thanksgiving feast. And, she was going to eat at all four feasts, as a greedy spider might do!

At long last Thanksgiving Day had arrived. Greedy Spider awoke and anxiously awaited the tugs at her waist— the signal that it was time to eat. But to her surprise, by noon, none had come. She was beginning to wonder if Mantis, Hamster, the two Snails, and Rabbit had tricked her because they were so jealous of her lovely home.

But that was not the case. Just before the afternoon, the first tug came from the two Snails. Finally, as she tried to loosen herself, the second tug came from Mantis, and the

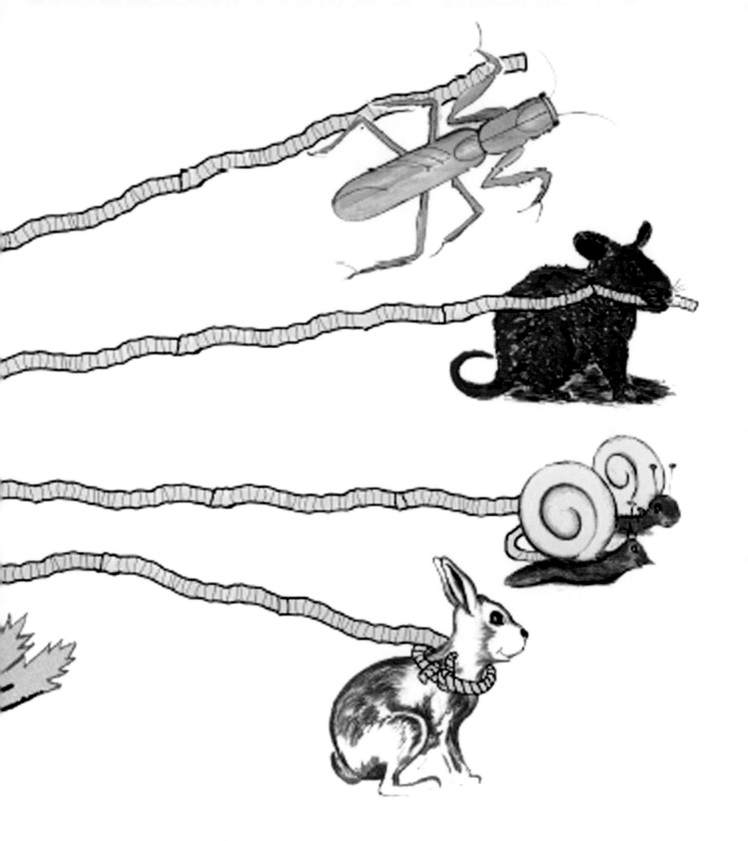

third tug came from Hamster, as Greedy
Spider began to breathe, the last one came
from Rabbit.

The ropes squeezed her waist so tightly that Greedy Spider gasped for air. What an awful dilemma! She could not call for help because all of her neighbors and friends were busy with their Thanksgiving feasts and no one would hear her pleas.

So, she could only sit and wait, hoping that soon someone would return home from their Thanksgiving feast and rescue her. But no one did.

By evening, Mantis decided that the Greedy Spider would not be joining his family for Thanksgiving dinner so, he bit the thread and released her. What a relief, whew!

An hour later, Hamster decided the same, so he gnawed the thread and released her. More relief!

An hour after that, the two Snails thought the same, so they chewed the thread and released her.

An hour after that, Rabbit reached the same conclusion, and chomped the thread of the rope and released her. The best relief!

Needless to say, Greedy Spider learned her lesson. From that day to this, she only accepts one invitation at a time. For all others, she graciously declines.

The End

Bakeh N. Wleh Nagbe, Sr.

Born in Liberia, Bakeh N. Wleh Nagbe, Sr. can remember hearing the Greedy Spider story first around the fire, then years later around a lantern. "The story is set in Nyantro, a small village on a rolling hill 55 miles outside Greenville, Sinoe County, Liberia. My grandfather has told and retold this story to me and the children of Nyantro. It was passed on to him after being handed down more than 700 years," says Nagbe.

Bakeh has been International Trade Specialist for Watdco with his experience he wrote his first book on international export and import management. Then decided to pen a children's book. His first manuscript was the story of the elephant and the chameleon. After much thought, Bakeh decided that the story of the Greedy Spider was more important. The thought that was most possessing in my childhood was the story of Greedy Spider, which my grand father told me and the children of Nyantro over and over again, year in year out.

Greedy Spider is the first in a series of four books. Bakeh now resides in Durham County, North Carolina and continues to work on his manuscripts.

Greedy Spider

This picture book is diligently written –designed, and constructed carefully with the children in mind. Greedy Spider is fun to read, it brings children, parents and grandparents together. The book, is the most tangible kids book, it provide hands on reading experience for any child. Speak directly to the children, and the kids respond enthusiastically to induce learning. We consider this book as the reading coach for all children. Not classics but a great storytelling, and the rewards are obvious.

Greedy Spider by BNW Nagbe, Sr., art by Melvin J. Carver, this book invites children to read. Greedy Spider will spark excitement in reading, and help kids relate better. This story is suitable for school as well as bedtime. When we buy something, we touch, smell, taste, feel, and test drive a car, well, we have pretested this book, and find it's to cover all children of 4 to 12 years of age or younger.

Glossary

prey (PR-praeda pre-hendered)
Prey to seize or devour and eating by powerful animals. One that is helpless and unable to resist attack or fight back
are the preys, and the powerful are the predators.

dilemma (DILE-mmatos)
Dilemma to make choice between two or more equally unsatisfactory situations, and choose the alternatives

chomp (CHO-champ)
Chomped is to chew or bite on something, either to eat or cut with teeth.

envy (EN-viable)
Envied feeling or showing envy, and to be jealous of your neighbor's success

gorgeous (GOR-gergia)
Gorgeous beautiful objects, a magnificent book or an elegant watch.

splendid (SPIEN-did)
Splendid shining things, superb or brilliantly arranged

sankontant (ZAN-kutent)
Spiders are called sankontant by the Kru tribes of Liberia.

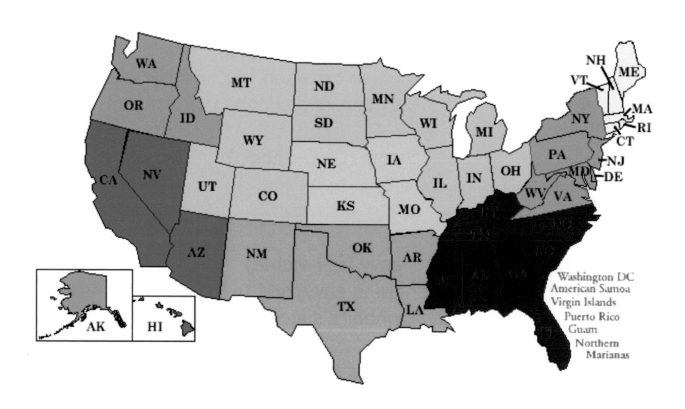

WA
MT
ND
MN
OR
ID
WI
SD
MI
NY
NH
VT
ME
MA
RI
CT
NJ
DE
PA
CA
NV
WY
UT
IA
IL
IN
OH
MD
WV
VA
CO
NE
KS
MO
AZ
NM
OK
AR
TX
LA
AK
HI

Washington DC
American Samoa
Virgin Islands
Puerto Rico
Guam
Northern
Marianas

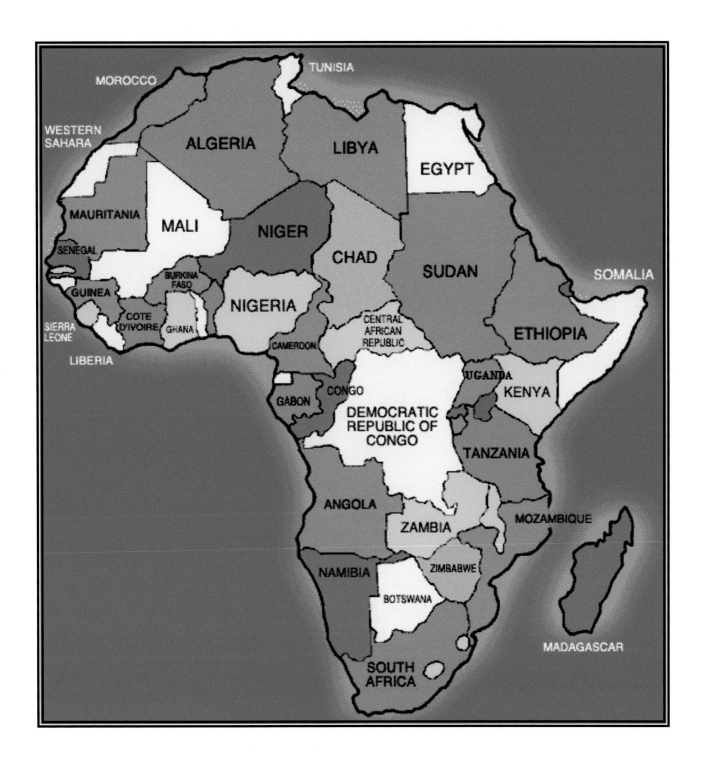

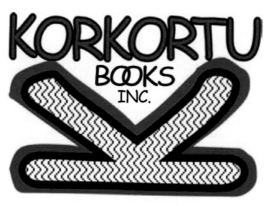

P.O. Box 25309
Durham, N.C. 27702
USA

Printed in the United States
By Bookmasters